How to Start Out or Over on a Shoestring

Other Titles by Annie Jean Brewer:

Nonfiction Titles:
The Shoestring Girl: How I Live on Practically
    Nothing...And YOU Can Too!
The Minimalist Cleaning Method
400 Ways to Save a Fortune
How to Watch Movies and Television Shows for Free
How to Write and Sell an Ebook
How to Write Ebooks For a Living
Where to Work Online
Professional Help: How to Prevent and Fix Malware,
    Viruses, Spyware and Other Baddies
How to Watch Stuff Online For Free
Be Happy Now
How to Be Happy

Fiction Titles:
163 Nights
The Bean Pot and Other Tales
What About Bob?

How to Start Out or Over on a Shoestring

Annie Jean Brewer

FIRST PRINT EDITION

Copyright 2012 by Annie Jean Brewer
Annienygma.com

PUBLISHED BY

Annie Jean Brewer on CreateSpace

Contents

To my daughter Katie.

Your love and companionship have seen me through the darkest days. This book could not have been written without you. I love you Katie Bug!

A Request

Please leave an honest review of this book at the website of your choice. This will help others like you determine if this book will help them. To thank you for your review I will be happy to send you a PDF copy of this book so that you can store it on your computer or print it out as desired. Please email me at annie@annienygma.com with a link to your published review and I will send you the PDF copy of this book.

Thank you!

Annienygma

Introduction

Embroiled in a custody battle that forced me to spend hours driving to court and other legal proceedings, I saw myself falling down a slippery slope of depression. My frustration grew as I watched a huge chunk of my income go into the gas tank of my van and into the refrigerators of friends who allowed me to crash at their place for the seemingly endless court dates.

Finally I had to acknowledge the futility of my actions. I was exhausted, stressed and quickly becoming financially challenged as gas prices went even higher. I decided to move back to the town that contained my past.

Rather than cry and scream at the injustice or deal with the fact that I would have to pay to haul my stuff, store it and then haul it again when I secured a place I made the choice to leave almost all of it behind. I gave the mobile home and possessions to a lady who had been homeless for a while, packed up what would fit in my van and drove away.

It occurred to me that my personal experience may help others who are starting out or, for whatever reason, have started over; by learning what you will need to just get started you will be freed from being overwhelmed and trying to remember everything at once.

This book may also help those who are planning to relocate to another area; by knowing the basics of what to keep you can be spared from making costly mistakes. I have learned a lot from this experience and it is my hope that sharing this knowledge will help others dealing with what can be an overwhelming situation.

This book was written from the viewpoint of someone who has started over on a shoestring but can be easily applied to someone just starting out. College, first apartment, relocation--there isn't any real difference because you will still need the basics to attain a level of comfort.

It's Just Stuff

Ingrained upon the American psyche is the belief that the more we have the more successful we are. The furniture, appliances, cars and gizmos we have are considered indicators of our status. When we encounter someone who has less than the standard amount of stuff we are shocked.

We immediately think that this person must have faced some sort of horrible disaster; surely no one in their right mind would *possibly* give up all of their stuff *willingly*? If they reveal that in fact they did willingly let go of their possessions, we think they must be insane!

Frankly, the typical Westerner is incredibly spoiled and has traveled so far from the simpler lifestyle in the past as to be unrecognizable. While there are a few possessions that we need, that number is far less than the average Westerner owns.

In 100 years the stuff that we own now will be worthless. The technology alone will become obsolete and far faster with the rest of our possessions trailing along behind. In this age of instant gratification and mass produced products our pressboard furniture and faux coverings are deliberately designed to wear out so that we are forced to buy even more.

Slavery

In order to purchase these things which will wear out, become obsolete or simply fall out of style we need to make enough money to pay for the goods as well as for numerous taxes. When you purchase on credit more hours must be spent paying the interest fees as well. Then we must pay to haul the stuff home, secure a larger home to hold the stuff, possibly rent a storage space to hold our excess and take even more time to care for these items that we have acquired.

Don't believe me? How many of you reading this spend your days off cleaning your house, organizing your garage or working a second job to pay your bills instead of relaxing and enjoying your life?

How many of you feel the need to upgrade your iPhone because Apple just released a new version, or to buy another computer because Microsoft has released a new version of Windows?

We are all becoming slaves to corporate America thanks to this rampant consumerism. Instead of enjoying our lives we spend it feeling insecure because we don't have the latest and greatest; or we are forced to work extra hours to pay for the upgrades and care for our overwhelming amount of possessions.

Starting Over = Freedom

When you are starting over for whatever reason you are freed from the need to care for all of those things. You have a slate wiped clean of possessions, enabling you to start over and only accumulate that which you actually need and will use.

No longer will you have to spend your days off organizing moldy boxes in the basement: instead you can spend your time doing things that you love to do.

When you look at things as if they are a big part of you it becomes painful when you have to part with your things for whatever reason, especially if you have to part with them unwillingly.

When you realize that most of your stuff is easily replaceable you become freed of the burden of keeping it with you or mourning its loss; you know that you can easily acquire more should you desire it.

A friend of mine lost most of his possessions after a move went awry. To this day he is still angry about the event. Whenever he thinks about the things he owned in the past, even if he replaced the item with something better, he rages about his loss. With every passing year he grows increasingly bitter instead of allowing himself to move on, even to the point where he hates discarding obvious trash because he fears "losing everything" again.

Don't let this be you. If, for whatever reason, you have to start over acknowledge the event, access what you DO have and move on. Focusing on what you lost will not bring your stuff back and it may prevent you from acquiring nicer things in the future!

Just Starting Out?

For those who are instead just starting out, you have an incredible advantage. You don't have the tons of clutter to bother with--just a few personal items. As you begin your journey remember to ask yourself if you really need that whatsit before you purchase. Just this one question can work wonders in preventing an overload of stuff.

Minimum Supplies

These lists contain the minimum supplies you will need to start over comfortably as you begin this new chapter in your life.

Some things may seem to be a bit overboard but if you have ever lived without these basics you will be thankful that you prepared! For instance, some houses and apartments do not come equipped with a refrigerator or stove; I have even seen some units without basic heating and cooling equipment! Having the basic equipment for this scenario will help you out immensely and can even benefit you if you are living with someone temporarily by providing you with your own personal space to keep food, drink, or even prepare food.

Items like a stove and a refrigerator are difficult and costly to come by in a pinch and their full size counterparts hard to move when you relocate; having smaller versions of these items on hand can greatly improve your options, especially if you don't have anyone to help you move!

Your next home may only have a single bowl sink or not come equipped with stoppers to hold water. Dish pans solve these issues and also enable to you reuse dishwater to flush the commode if you have to wait to get the water turned on. You can also use these dishpans to clean other areas of your house or to carry items if needed.

If you have enough money to purchase an air mattress, go to a used furniture store and invest in a bed instead. If not, grab a sleeping bag from your local discount store for around twenty bucks and rest content in the fact that you won't have to wake up to life on a deflating air pocket!

It is assumed by the author that once you get situated and have a steady income that you will undoubtedly upgrade from the items listed on these pages; this author would be disappointed if you did not upgrade to more comfortable items in the areas that you feel a need as the money and opportunity arises.

When starting out it can be hard to determine what you need; all you can consider is that you need "everything." These lists are written in hopes to give you a start; a basic list to focus upon and a foundation while you are feeling overwhelmed.

Swallow Your Pride

When it comes time to start out, take your pride and toss it in a dumpster somewhere. The only thing pride will do at a time like this is cause you discomfort and upset. You cannot afford the cost of pride, so get rid of it!

You may need to accept the charity of others during this time; be thankful that there are others who care about you and accept any and all help graciously. Do not gripe because something isn't your favorite color or has a small scratch; if it works and does the job you need it to do then accept it and be thankful.

There may be some who distance themselves from you simply because they cannot associate with that you are experiencing; these will most likely be the ones from your old work, your old church--your old station in life. They may not do this to be mean but it will hurt nevertheless; it is easier if you are the one who makes the conscious break and moves on instead. This will be the time when you discover who your TRUE friends are!

Be Grateful

Be grateful that you have your life and your health; that you have the ability to start over despite any and all challenges you may face.

Be happy that you have discovered a book that will help you learn what you will need while you are starting out.

Above all dismiss negativity from your life. Dwelling on what don't have will accomplish nothing and will bring bitterness in its' stead; focus on the new life, the new stuff and the new experiences that you are immersing yourself within!

Have a Good Cry

If you feel the need just go off somewhere so that you can be entirely alone and have a good cry. Beat some pillows, rip up some grass, break some sticks, and toss some rocks. Scream if you can do so without arousing undue attention, but release those emotions so that you can get on with your life. We all have feelings but we don't need to let them control us.

Use What You Have and Find

At first it will seem as if you need supplies wherever you turn and this may cause you to panic.

Relax--you have just enough to get started, and more will come as needed.

For instance, cut the top off of a soft drink bottle to create a funnel.

- Reuse plastic lunch meat and deli tubs to store leftovers and other items.
- Plastic grocery bags can get a second life as trash and storage bags.
- Stained clothing can be cut up and used as towels and cleaning cloths.
- Gallon milk and water jugs can be used to store your first batches of dishwashing liquid, laundry soap and liquid hand soap. Cut one in half at an angle and you will have a handled scoop that will double as a funnel as well. Cut off the bottom and you have a bowl for yourself or your pets. Fill them with cold drinking water or use them to hold lemonade or other drinks.
- Empty take out cups can be used to store things like pencils or other items and cereal boxes can be cut and used to store papers and magazines.
- A piece of thick paper can be used in place of a dust pan.

- A tallish box lined with a grocery bag becomes a trash can.
- A discarded toothbrush becomes a scrub brush and is excellent for cleaning small spaces.
- A ragged bath towel can be cut into strips and attached to the bottom of a handle (or any long stick) with wire or zip ties to make a mop.
- Hooks and wire or string can be used to make curtain rods or to hang shower curtains. You can even use thumb tacks or staples to attach curtains at first!
- A simple piece of rope becomes a clothesline wherever you choose to hang it.
- Old compact discs can be used as coasters.
- Plastic margarine tubs; gallon jugs and similar items can be used as flowerpots.
- Metal cans with the top cut off become storage for pencils, silverware or other items.
- Metal cans with the top and bottom removed become biscuit and cookie cutters. Tuna fish cans make the best biscuit and cookie cutters--they are heavy duty and virtually free!
- Sheets and other pieces of fabric can become curtains. Secure the fabric to the window with push pins at the top or drape over a curtain rod.
- Small metal cans with sand in the bottom can hold candles or incense safely while burning.
- Plastic container lids can become spoon rests, coasters, drip catchers, Frisbees or other things.
- Shallow cans like tuna fish cans make great ash trays.

- Jars can store anything from dried beans to buttons.

Just because something wasn't bought from the store to serve a particular purpose does not mean that it cannot be used that way.

Old pieces of leather can become a hinge; a piece of wood and a nail can become a door (or gate) latch.

Anything is possible when you think out of the box that consumerism has pushed you in, so before you discard something while you are starting out, look at it and make a game of discovering new uses for that item.

Money

When starting out money is essential. Eliminate all of your extra expenses during this period. Don't worry--the spending fast is just until you get back on your feet!

Bank Accounts

Of primary importance is the ability to generate income but bank accounts are important too. Money is useful only if you have a way to cash the checks!

Brick and Mortar

Brick and Mortar banks are the ones you see on every street corner. They are the physical banks that have been around for hundreds of years. While check cashing and payday loan places provide some of the services that traditional brick and mortar banks provide, this is the place that will safely store your money until you need to use it. Most banks are insured, but if you happen to see a bank that isn't think twice about trusting them with your money.

At the very least you will need to open up a checking account at a brick and mortar bank and you can use that account to hold spare change that you save up or whatever. Most banks provide you with a debit/credit card that you can use to pay with instead of checks as well.

PayPal

If you decide to work at an online business a PayPal account will be an essential. Large numbers of places are only able to pay to PayPal accounts, so having one set up is to your advantage. Go to www.paypal.com to set up your free PayPal account. Note that some accounts will provide you with a debit card that can be used as a credit card, allowing you to get cash back on your purchases. This money adds up if you use the card very often.

Employment

Once you have your bank accounts set up it will be time to start looking for work. Ask people you know if anyone is hiring for even temporary work. Some of these jobs will pay cash money, leaving it up to you to report your earnings to the Tax Man.

Search online for jobs that may interest you. They may be boring but they will pay the bills. Some like CloudCrowd only have work on a sporadic basis depending upon your qualifications but others like MTurk have simple jobs all of the time that people can do. For a huge list of places that accept online workers, check out the book Where to Work Online[1]. This book features both traditional and freelance positions that are available to the home-based worker.

If you can write, consider opening an account at the Yahoo Contributor Network. Formerly known as Associated Content, this site not only pays upfront for certain types of articles but will pay you a bonus on the amount of pageviews you receive as well. You pageview rate will go up based on how many articles you publish and how many total pageviews you receive, and you have the chance of being featured on the main Yahoo website.

Starting a blog can not only help to relieve stress by providing an outlet but it can also provide an income as well. Writing about subjects that interest you, you can place affiliate links within your material that will earn you a sales commission should your readers purchase an item using your link.

---

[1] http://www.amazon.com/Where-to-Work-Online-ebook/dp/B004BLJAP0/ref=sr_1_1?ie=UTF8&qid=135018 6376&sr=8-1&keywords=where+to+work+online

You can also create an ebook, recording or other creation of your own and sell it on your blog. These creations can provide you with a residual income that lasts long after you hit the publish button. Check out <u>How to Write and Sell an Ebook</u>[2] for more information.

The Public Job

There is nothing wrong with getting a public job. Anything that pays the bills is honorable work and should not be discounted.

At first you cannot afford to be picky; it is a well-known fact that employed people are more desirable to hiring managers than unemployed ones so if you don't have a job apply everywhere until you get one.

If you have any type of freelance experience use that on your job applications to qualify as being currently employed; it is better to be a self-employed housecleaner (who rarely accepts jobs) than it is to be an unemployed CEO! Make sure it is something you have experience in however; employers may ask you to describe experiences from your self-employment!

---

[2] http://www.amazon.com/How-Write-Sell-Ebook-ebook/dp/B00413PW2I/ref=la_B009EXAB1W_1_12?ie=UTF8&qid=1350186457&sr=1-12

When applying for public jobs keep your appearance neat and clean. Hide the tats and piercings unless you are applying for a position where they could be considered of benefit. Let's be blunt: if two people are applying for one job, the clean-cut person will get it EVEN if the one covered in tats or piercings is more qualified. It isn't fair but that is how it is. Play the game and you will land a job. Refuse and you may starve.

Always be on time (or a little early) for any interviews or appointments, and ALWAYS dress neatly. Keep the personal chatter to a minimum but be friendly. Just get the job, any job and then worry about applying for something that pays more (or is more to your liking).

Create Your Own Job

While you are searching for employment make your own job. Wash windows, fix whatsits, clean houses, babysit, mow lawns--ask around for anyone needing odd jobs completed and negotiate a reasonable wage. Depending upon the area (and task) $10 an hour is considered fair wages for most odd jobs.

Farmers frequently need someone to help with hay or other crops, so visit the local farmers to see if they need help for a few days. Apartment owners and construction crews sometimes need people to clean up after tenants and new construction so you can contact them as well. Visit your local realtors to see if they know of any rentals or houses for sale in need of a good cleaning. Banks sometimes will hire people to clean out foreclosed homes, so don't forget to inquire there as well.

Grab some cloths, a squeegee, a little dishwashing liquid and some water then visit the local businesses. Ask them if they need their windows cleaned and quote them a reasonable price. Offer to wash a window for free so that they can see the quality of your work. You may end up with a regular clientele of customers and not NEED to find a public job! I know one gentleman who washed windows while he traveled cross country-- just enough in each town for gas and food so that he could travel to the next. You could do this, or just make enough in one town to pay your bills.

Offer to wash cars while their owners are at work or do simple maintenance like oil changes if you have the skills to do so. Anything is possible if you have simple skills!

If you like animals offer your services as a pet sitter at the local veterinarians and pet groomers; you can even offer to clean up pet waste in yards or scoop out litter boxes for harried pet owners. Post a sign offering these and other pet-related services at local animal-related businesses.

Sell Stuff

If you aren't too proud to dumpster dive check the dumpsters of apartment complexes and businesses for things you can sell at flea markets or on Craigslist. Checking the curbs on trash pickup day (especially around holidays) can net you some big ticket items that are no longer wanted by the original owners. I have known some people with a little money who would visit auctions and purchase items for almost nothing (boxes and lots for a buck or two) and sell the stuff for a profit. Once we purchased a truck load of old bed frames for $2 and sold the frames individually for $5 apiece! Anything is possible if you can purchase it for cheap!

I have taken old computer parts that were given to me and assembled functional computer systems and sold them for a profit. If you have computer skills you can do this as well with a little time and patience.

Annie Jean Brewer

Do Whatever It Takes

Do whatever it takes to pay the bills until you land a steady income. Don't worry--you will be okay!

Transportation

If you have access to a car--great. If not, use a bicycle, walk or rely on public transportation to get started.

Honestly, if you have a large car payment you may be better off eliminating the car (and the payment) while you get back on your feet. Fewer payments are always better for those who are starting out. Used cars can be found in the local classifieds for less (sometimes significantly so) than a thousand dollars, so use your judgment when getting back on your feet.

Discard the notion that you "have" to have a car. You don't: a car is a luxury in most urban areas, while it may be a necessity if you live in the country. People were getting by on foot for thousands of years before the car was invented and even today billions of people worldwide are doing just fine without a car.

You can rent or borrow a vehicle when you need to haul large stuff, but otherwise use what you already have and be thankful that you have legs to carry you.

Even if you do have a car keep it parked as much as possible while you get back on your feet. This will save on gas and maintenance for the vehicle and possibly delay and repairs that might need to be done. Walk, bike or use public transportation as much as you can and carpool to work if it is available.

Remember that reducing or eliminating the expense of a car will greatly improve your finances. For instance, while my van is paid off I still have to pay approximately $500 a year for car insurance, $60 for tags and a couple hundred dollars (or more) a year for maintenance and repairs. In my personal experience, you will spend approximately $500 a year on maintenance and repairs on an older vehicle, more if you need a complete set of tires. This may be significantly less than if one had a car payment, but one can easily save $100 a month by not having a car at all in just maintenance, repairs, insurance and other fees--not including gasoline.

One Advantage to Having a Vehicle

There is one advantage to owning a vehicle: you can live in it while you get back on your feet. Check out the section on housing for more information.

Housing

Put your pride on a shelf when searching for your first place; do not consider yourself too good for any home and base each place on its own merits.

You may have to stay in a shelter at first; they aren't perfect but it is better than no home at all. Keep any money close to your person; an excellent place to stash cash money is the bottom of your sock near your heel. It won't bother you much as you walk and most thieves won't think about someone keeping money there. Wherever you hide your money, don't tell anyone where you have it hidden, and don't advertise that you have any cash at all!

Staying with family and friends is another option while you get back on your feet. Generally they won't ask for money (if they do, it won't be much), and this will allow you to save any money that you earn so that you can get back on your feet.

Living With Others

If you do have to stay with others for a time do everything in your power to make it as easy and pleasant on them. The goal is to have them miss you when you are gone so that they have good feelings about the experience of helping you.

Regardless of whether or not they ask, work to contribute money toward the household expenses. Offer it to them even if they don't accept; you may not be able to pitch in much money and they may even refuse, but the fact that you show your willingness to help out will go a long ways toward harmony with your hosts.

Buy groceries and supplies for the household as money allows. You may only be able to afford to help with some soft drinks or cleaning supplies but every little bit that you contribute moves you from being a mooch to being a welcome member of the household.

Do things around the house to help out like washing dishes, laundry and general house cleaning. You don't have to go overboard, but the easier that you make their life the smoother things will be. This is especially important if you are unable to contribute financially to the household expenses.

Try not to hog limited resources. For instance, if you enjoy long baths, schedule them for when everyone is gone or asleep so that you can still do something that you enjoy but it won't intrude upon their routine.

ALWAYS pick up after yourself and clean up any mess that you make. If you use something, put it back where they placed it immediately when you are done. Messy guests are a huge annoyance and neatnik habits in this case may allow you to extend your visit some to better get back on your feet financially.

Shelters

At first you may have to stay in a shelter while securing more permanent housing; if this is the case find a safe location to store your supplies; shelters are notorious for theft. This is one situation where renting a small storage building will actually be of benefit; you can collect the items you need for your future home without worrying about moving them daily for the check-in/checkout regulations that shelters apply.

Hide any money you have in your socks, keep it in a bank or hidden somewhere. Do NOT tell anyone around you that you have so much as two pennies to rub together--it may get you robbed or beaten in your sleep. Don't spend money around

31

your fellow shelter residents. This is a giant tip-off to others that you are not as broke as you seem. Let everyone think you are broke and desperate, if not a little dangerous.

Be scrupulously clean to avoid catching any stray germs and follow all of the shelter's rules and regulations. Do what you can to escape notice and work hard to procure safer housing. Above all don't lose hope: Chris Gardner himself lived with his young son in a series of shelters and on the street before he made it big; check out the movie "In Pursuit of Happyness" to see for yourself.

VanDwelling

If you have a vehicle, congratulate yourself at this point. You can never be truly homeless so long as you have a vehicle!

VanDwelling is the art of living in vehicles. This has been practiced by retirees and free spirits for ages. Think back to the Gypsy wagons of ancient times, or the traveling caravans of carnival workers to see the potential available to you.

Living discreetly in your vehicle can provide you with a safe haven while you are searching for more traditional digs. Vans and recreational vehicles are the best for this but many have lived successfully in small pickup trucks equipped with camper tops and even small cars. Visit the Cheap RV living website listed in the References section for more information

I have personally lived in my van for short camping trips with the kid or while traveling to and from court dates during my years-long custody battle. If you keep a low profile it can actually be a pleasant

VanDwelling Commode

One thing of note if you decide to live in your vehicle for a short time: bathrooms. Instead of investing in a portable toilet, get a small bucket (5 gallon buckets are ideal), some trash bags (grocery bags work in a pinch), toilet paper and scented clumping kitty litter. Line the bucket with a couple of trash bags and pour some kitty litter inside. Do your business and cover with more kitty litter until your waste cannot be identified. Tie the bag up and discard in a nearby trash receptacle. The clumping litter will protect others (and you), the scent will disguise the contents (most will think it is traditional cat waste) and you will be able to use the bathroom in your vehicle without having to suffer if a bathroom is not in sight!

Renting/Owning

Go cheap for your first home so that you can get out on your own faster. This may be a room rented by the week or a whole house secured inexpensively because of location and/or poor condition. The goal is not to have a perfect place, but to just have a place. You are in the process of moving up so relax in the knowledge that you will not be stuck with the imperfections.

Keep your pride on a shelf for this first place; it is far more important that you regain your independence than to worry about where the Jones' are living. Do not consider yourself too "good" for any home or location: consider every single place on its own individual merits.

In some cases you may be able to secure the ownership of an older mobile home for less than it costs to rent an apartment. I have personally purchased older mobile homes for less than a thousand dollars; the last home I even swapped some of my furniture towards the purchase price! You may still have to pay rent on the lot the home sits upon but if you find yourself needing close to $1,000 just to move into an apartment why not consider using that money to purchase a home instead?

Older Mobile Homes can be purchased inexpensively

Furniture

You don't need a lot of furniture when you are starting over on a shoestring, despite what everyone will tell you. Truth be told you really don't need *any* if you can handle sitting on the floor!

Bare Basics

The bare basics you really need are:
- Sleeping bag
- Extra blankets for cold weather
- Sheet to sleep under in warm weather
- Pillow

You can both sit and sleep on a sleeping bag or graduate to a futon if you have one available. When I moved into my new place, all I had at first was a sleeping bag, a couple of blankets and a borrowed pillow until I could get my stuff moved down from my cousin's house where it was stored.

Sleeping bag, blanket and pillow I used when I first moved to my new place.

Some of you will scoff at the fact that instead of a bed I have listed a sleeping bag. It is much easier to acquire and move a sleeping bag when you are starting over than it is to acquire and move a big heavy bed. Once you get situated you can get whatever bed you desire but for starting out go with the basics. You need a place to sleep, not a giant four-poster!

What About An Air Mattress?

Some will declare that instead of a sleeping bag it is much better to get an air mattress. Air mattresses can cost as much as a used bed but are not near as sturdy. One slight mishap: a dropped match, sitting on your keys, even an enthusiastic pet can completely destroy an air mattress faster than it took you to earn the money to purchase it!

I recommend some sort of table and chairs if you have one available. I kept a coffee table from my childhood and that saw me through until I located a kitchen table and some chairs. Guests tend to be uncomfortable when you ask them to sit on the floor or on pillows; you can also more readily work on things if you have a table to use.

Anything else, like a couch, official bed and other items can be accumulated as time goes on. People will go out of their way to try to outfit you when you show off your new place so furniture will come quickly and easily. I have to politely refuse a lot of items that are offered out of a sense of generosity, and you will too!

Housewares

Housewares are one section where you will need multiple items to get started comfortably. While there may be some who say that you can start with a bowl and a spork the majority of us prefer a bit more to life than that provides!

For each person's personal use I recommend at the minimum:

- One plate
- One bowl
- One saucer (also doubles as a coaster on furniture)
- One cup
- One fork
- One teaspoon
- One knife
- One napkin (bandannas are great for this, but you can also use paper towels)

This doesn't leave a lot of room for play but it gets the job done when you're starting out. Don't worry at this point about any of it matching. As long as it serves the purpose you will get by.

The Kitchen

There are other items that you will need to round out your kitchen. Failure to stock these items may result in you having to outsource your cooking at the local fast food dive! I'm just kidding about that, but these items make cooking a lot easier:

- Mixing bowl
- 1-2 pans with lids for cooking (oven safe pans can double as baking pans)
- 1 oven safe skillet (it will double as a baking pan at first)
- Spatula
- Wooden spoon (2 recommended)
- Kitchen knife
- Cutting board (the inexpensive plastic ones are perfect)
- Measuring cup
- 1 tablespoon
- 2 dishpans for washing yourself, clothes, dishes or other items as needed

Food

Food is a difficult list to make because all of us have different preferences and tastes. Some of you will prefer lunch meat for sandwiches, or enjoy eating ramen noodles all of the time, while others love seafood and more exotic fare.

Some of us eat a more country fare, and still others may live in other countries and prefer foods that I may have never heard of. For an in-depth look at stocking a minimalist kitchen (and what to do once you stock it) I highly recommend Minimalist Cooking by Meg Wolfe[3]. She not only covers what to stock in a basic kitchen (food and all) but how to prepare 27 different items.

Honestly folks, I'm not much of a cook. I read Meg's book to learn how to do what little cooking I do, so I will simply recommend her book and leave you to an expert instead of taking the chance of guiding you wrong.

Other Items

Here are a few more items you will need to round out your collection:

- 1-2 towels per person for bathing, drying hands
- 1-2 wash cloths per person
- Small assortment of rags for cleaning and drying. These can be cut from discarded towels and clothing. If you want to be tidy, apply super glue, nail glue or Fray Check the edges to prevent fraying.
- Pair of scissors
- Matches or a cigarette lighter
- Flashlight

---

[3] http://minimalistcook.com/minimalist-cooking/

- Cord or thin rope (clothesline)
- Chair that can double as a step stool
- Super glue (for repairs)
- Duct tape (for repairs)
- Sewing needle
- Transparent sewing thread (for repairs on clothing).
- Box of light bulbs

Electronics

You really only need two pieces of electronic equipment to get by but three pieces are best:

- Laptop with Wi-Fi capability
- Headset with microphone built-in
- Cell phone

A laptop can be used as a stereo, television, book reader, email device and telephone with Gmail's Google Voice feature. You can also use a MagicJack[4] for $29 a year to make phone calls on your computer as well, using a traditional landline phone, but if you decide to use Skype, Google Voice or other computer-based VOIP phone service you will need the headset to make phone calls.

A cell phone is optional but can be used for text messaging as well as for an alarm clock. Its mobility and small size make it an ideal addition, and with prepaid cell phones costing as low as $20 for a phone and starter service it is a worthwhile investment.

---

[4] http://www.magicjack.com/plus-v05/

I keep a prepaid cell phone but I mainly use it for text messaging and as a personal alarm clock. Most cell phones also contain a calculator and a memo application so you can save paper and use it for small lists. Otherwise I use my laptop and MagicJack to make phone calls wherever I can access the internet, be it at home or at a wireless hotspot.

A wireless internet connection converts a simple laptop into a variety of devices and can save the average user a small fortune every month. Instead of a television and cable subscription you can use a Wi-Fi connection to watch television at sites like Hulu and others.

Instead of a radio you can visit sites like Pandora for internet radio.

Instead of having shelves of books, the Kindle app and other e-reader programs enable you to have an entire library of books stashed on your hard drive.

Instead of a monthly phone bill, you can use your laptop's Wi-Fi connection to make and receive phone calls.

This laptop doesn't have to be the latest and greatest to save you a fortune in space and money.

Just a basic laptop with a DVD drive and Wi-Fi capability will work just fine to watch movies, television shows and do other things with.

I use my laptop for all of these things and even more. It has replaced my home phone, television, cable subscription, physical library, stereo, planner and many other things. The machine is truly a game-changer when it comes to starting over on a shoestring.

Appliances

There is a short list of appliances that you will need while you get started. Possession of these pieces will mean that you are able to rent places that do not come equipped with a stove and refrigerator--saving you money as you start out, for you can negotiate a lower rent in places that do not include these pieces.

- Hot plate (2 burner recommended)
- Refrigerator. Any size, even a dorm size will work. You can even use a cooler and ice at first if needed. I started out using a cooler and graduated to an under-counter refrigerator in this house--the freezer is small but sufficient for one or two people.
- Microwave.
- Toaster oven.
- 1 lamp per person to use at night when reading, etc.
- Portable heater for areas that are cold in the winter.
- Small air conditioner (recommended).

These are the bare basics to provide for your needs in almost any place you end up. The hot plate, microwave and toaster oven are smaller but capable of being used in place of a larger range, which means that you won't have to worry about hauling or storing a full size range while you get settled. You can also use those items regardless of whether or not you acquire a range so they will come in handy regardless.

Refrigerator, Microwave and Toaster Oven With a Hot Plate on the countertop

You will need a way to keep some things cold and while a cooler and ice can be used at first the so-called "dorm" refrigerators are used in several countries as standard refrigeration units. They hold enough to get by with no excess space for leftovers to hide and go bad. You may have to shop a bit more often but your food will be fresher and you will be able to enjoy a good variety, and you won't have to worry about moving your small refrigerator: even the larger dorm refrigerators are small enough for a single person to move in a car.

Another serious advantage of "dorm" refrigerators is cost. In many areas it is considerably cheaper to purchase a new "dorm" refrigerator with a warranty than it is to purchase a used full-size refrigerator *without* a warranty! In my personal case I decided to use one of these small devices as my permanent refrigeration unit because of price and space considerations.

Later on if you desire you can supplement your small refrigerator with a small chest freezer, but this is not a necessity while you are getting started.

If you can acquire an inexpensive small chest freezer first, you can use it to freeze ice in containers to keep items cool in a freezer. This allows you to have the benefit of owning two appliances with the electricity usage of only a single device. I did this personally when I first moved into the home I rented. Just remember to swap out the ice containers with frozen ones on a daily basis and you are set!

Some really cheap rentals don't have heating or air conditioning built in so if you own your own heating and cooling appliances it can really help out. I not only keep a couple of small electric heaters but a small kerosene heater to heat with in the event of a power outage or other unexpected event. In a pinch you can heat or cool just a single room until you can make other arrangements. I do that personally even now when I am by myself to save extra money by closing off rooms that I'm not using.

Clothing

A few pieces of clothing can go a long way.

Seriously.

There is even a project where someone wore the same black dress every day for a year! Check out the Uniform Project[5] for more information.

You don't need a closet full of clothes when you are starting over--just a few outfits will do. Depending upon your line of work, you can get by with as little as four outfits by rotating them between wearings and washing them when dirty in your sink then hanging them up to dry. You can even stretch them and visit a Laundromat once a week if you have the money to afford the expense.

Air out your clothing between wearings: this will extend the amount of time before you have to wash them, especially if you are careful to avoid getting them dirty. I normally rotate between two to four outfits each week and visit the laundry weekly to clean them. You will also have the added benefit of

---

[5] http://www.theuniformproject.com/

longer lasting clothes, for using the washer and dryer shortens the life of the fibers.

You will need at least one dress outfit for job interviews, court appearances and other important occasions. If you go timeless with this outfit, like a standard gray suit or a little black dress you won't have to worry about changing trends--you will always be in style!

Shoes

I recommend one pair of dress casual shoes--you want a pair that you can dress up or down with ease and wear comfortably all day. For ladies that may be a pair of black flats and for men that may be a pair of simple loafers. Forget the trendy tennis shoes and stripper heels. You can splurge on those when you get back on your feet!

Underclothing and Night Wear

Keep extra underclothing on hand, at least 8-10 day's worth of changes. One never knows what can happen and you may run behind on your laundry. The extra underwear will enable to you change these items every day without issue even if it takes you an extra day or so before you can do laundry!

Oversized tee shirts work well for sleeping and make comfortable nightgowns for ladies. Combine that with a pair of comfy boxer shorts and you have a good all-around sleepwear outfit for both genders. I have some pajama bottoms from old fashioned pajamas that I have paired with tee shirts for an updated sleepwear look at a cost of nothing, as both the tee shirts and pajama bottoms were hand-me-downs.

How to Shop for Clothing

Watch the clearance sections at stores like Wal-Mart, Target, Kmart and other places. Sometimes you can pick up new items of clothing for less than you can purchase them used at a thrift store. I have bought brand new jeans, sweatshirts, pants and other items for $1 an item by shopping the clearance sections, but remember to only purchase what you can actually use and that will fit! It isn't a bargain if you already own too many already, or it is too small to squeeze into!

Thrift shops like Goodwill stores are another wonderful place to find clothing and other items you may need. You can find wonderful bargains there if you just look. I have not only purchased additions to my wardrobe in thrift stores, but shoes, blankets, appliances and other essential items at rock bottom prices--all in perfectly good condition. If you are squeamish about buying used, remind yourself that you are helping the environment by decreasing the amount of stuff that will hit the landfills!

Friends and family are another great source for clothing, particularly among females. If you happen to have someone in your circle who loves clothing you can almost rest assured that they will offer you a bag of clothing at some point. Accept it graciously and enjoy the treasures that you find within!

Personal Care

You don't need a lot of personal care items to start out. To my surprise it actually takes very little to maintain cleanliness. One does not *need* makeup; it is a luxury. That said, some will still insist upon adding cosmetics to this list but I do not include them here:

- Bar of Soap
- Toothbrush
- Toothpaste
- Dental Floss
- Deodorant
- Shampoo (Shampoo/conditioner combination recommended but not necessary)
- Nail Clippers
- Hair Brush
- Sanitary Pads or Tampons (ladies)
- Bathroom Tissue

Go with smaller sizes and generic brands to save money at first; you can buy the fancier stuff when you have the money to spare.

The Truth About Cleaning Supplies

I have a confession to make when it comes to cleaning supplies.

You don't need most of them.

Seriously.

The advent of microfiber has totally revolutionized cleaning. All you really need for most jobs now is a microfiber cloth and some water--and sometimes you don't even need the water.

You can clean windows with a damp microfiber cloth and a dry microfiber cloth. Wipe with the damp one and dry with the other one. This will give you a streak-free shine.

You can even use this on computer monitors, exteriors--almost anything that you want to clean.

If it's a little dirtier than a regular microfiber cloth can handle, break out the "Magic" Eraser. Add a little water and you can clean countless MORE items.

So, if you HONESTLY want to clean your house on a shoestring, schlep over to the local Family Dollar and grab a bag of microfiber cloths. They generally keep the bulk bags of random pieces over in the Automotive department for around five bucks. That is cheaper than you can buy the fancy packs and they contain enough variety in sizes to handle any job you need them to do.

Heck, I even use them to clean and dry *me*.

If you still want to use traditional cleaning methods, keep reading. I have a bunch of tips and recipes to save you some money.

Cleaning Supplies and Tips

*"It ain't no sin to be poor; soap and water don't cost **that** much!"*
-Orpha Brewer

As Grandmother used to say: "Soap and water don't cost that much." However that is hard to tell from the prices you find in the cleaning supplies aisle at the local market. Frankly, the prices are outrageous and you don't need hardly anything from that aisle anyway!

Here is a list of basic cleaning supplies. This will enable you to clean almost anything in your home and will cost a fraction of the price of the fancy stuff. Remember, you are just starting out so don't worry about going high class--just worry about getting the job done!

If you would like more tips and recipes, check out the bestselling book <u>The Minimalist Cleaning Method</u>[6].

Disclaimer:
To be safe, test everything on an inconspicuous spot before using. I am not your mother and therefore will be responsible for any mishaps.

Physical Supplies

- Broom
- Dustpan
- Mop
- Scrub brush
- Scrub pads
- Assorted rags
- Sponge (optional)
- Trash bags (can use repurposed grocery bags)
- Commode brush
- Bucket
- Dishpan (use one of the pans you picked up in the Housewares section)
- "Magic" erasers (grab the generic ones, they work just as well)

Cleaners

- Ammonia
- Water
- Bleach
- Octagon soap (comes in bars)

---

[6] http://www.amazon.com/Minimalist-Cleaning-Expanded-Edition-ebook/dp/B0095B6ENW/ref=sr_1_1?s=digital-text&ie=UTF8&qid=1350216925&sr=1-1&keywords=minimalist+cleaning+method

- Baking soda
- Washing soda (sodium carbonate, sold under the name of Arm and Hammer Washing Soda or can also be found in the pool care section under the name of "PH Raiser" - just verify that the main ingredient is sodium carbonate)
- Borax

That is all you need to clean your whole house, car, or whatever, so you can pass all of those fancy cleaners on by and keep that money in your pocket. This will even wash your laundry and your dishes!

Basic Cleaning Supplies

Ammonia

Ammonia is one of the best all-purpose cleaners available on the market. It is cheap at approximately $1 for a half gallon but can be used to clean walls, floors, woodwork, carpeting, laundry, commodes, tubs, showers, bathrooms, ovens, windows and almost anything else you will encounter.

Ammonia does not require rinsing which means that you are saved an extra cleaning step when compared to regular soaps, and in fact is the primary ingredient in many of the more expensive cleaners on the market. They dilute it, add some perfume and a bit of color and then market it under a fancy name to make the average person think they are getting something special, when in fact all they are *really* getting is a bottle of diluted ammonia in some fancy packaging!

How to Use Ammonia

To use ammonia in general cleaning applications place 1/2 cup of ammonia into a gallon of warm water. Always ventilate the area where you use ammonia, for the fumes can be very strong and may be unpleasant to some.

For safety, never mix ammonia with other chemicals like bleach. You can mix it with some soaps safely, but when mixed with bleach a gas is produced that is very dangerous.

Dampen your cloth or sponge with this solution and scrub until clean, using a scrub brush as needed. Rinse the cloth (sponge) and brush as needed when they become dirty and change your cleaning solution when the liquid becomes dirty.

For heavy duty dirt use 1 cup of ammonia per gallon of water in your cleaning solution. You can use ammonia up to full strength in really dirty cleaning jobs--just test a small spot first for safety, because ammonia is very powerful.

Ovens

To clean ovens, warm the oven and then place a bowl of ammonia inside. Close the door and leave there overnight. The fumes will penetrate the burned-on debris and enable you to clean the oven much easier. Wash the walls of the oven down the next day in a solution of 1 cup of ammonia (use the ammonia you placed in the bowl) per 1/2 gallon of water, changing the water as needed.

Windows

To clean windows create a basic ammonia solution. Wash windows with this solution using a clean cloth and then dry with paper towels or lint free cloths.

Floors

To wash floors create a basic ammonia solution and mop with this solution. Test a small area of your floor first for safety. If in doubt, wash with plain warm water or make a solution of 1 cup vinegar per gallon of water instead. You can also simply reduce the ammonia in the basic solution to 1/4 cup per gallon of water to make a very mild solution that should be safe on almost all surfaces.

Clean and Freshen Carpets

To freshen carpets sprinkle baking soda or borax on them and sweep in. Allow to sit on the carpet for at least an hour (I leave mine in for a day or more) before sweeping it back up.

Borax or baking soda will absorb dirt and odors from your carpets, but borax provides a bit of insect control as well. Borax is related to boric acid and is hazardous to insects when they lick it off of their feet after walking over it. If you are worried about insects just leave a little borax on your carpets at all times. Just reapply and sweep into the carpet pile after you clean your floors.

Vacuum Cleaners

Contrary to popular opinion one does not need a vacuum cleaner to clean carpets. In fact, carpets were originally kept clean by sweeping with a broom. During spring cleaning the carpets were removed from the home and scrubbed well with an ammonia and water solution. They were hung out to dry before being placed back in the home.

When starting over do not bother with a vacuum cleaner at first unless you can borrow one easily or find a machine for free of very cheap. You can keep your carpets clean without it.

Carpet Sweeping

In today's age of gadget dependence the art of sweeping carpets has been all but lost. Manufacturers have worked to convince us that we have to own a super-suction vacuum cleaner and a heavy-duty shampooer in order to keep our carpets looking their best.

While these gadgets are nice to have the odds of you actually having access to these items while starting over are slim; frankly you have more important things to spend your money on while you are getting on your feet. Learning to clean your carpets the old-fashioned way will allow you to have a clean floor without the expense of additional gadgets during the time when you cannot afford additional expenses.

Start at the far corner of the room that you wish to sweep. Lightly brush the broom across the surface of the carpet in the general direction of the door. It may take a few swipes of the broom to find the right combination of pressure and speed for your particular carpet pile, but keep trying and you will start to see the dirt move.

Sweep the carpet completely and use a dust pan to sweep the debris into when you finish the room. If you have one available (don't go out and buy one) use a portable hand vac to suction up the dirt to save time over sweeping it into a dustpan.

Carpet Mopping

Another thing you can do to keep your carpets their cleanest is mop them. In my personal experience, regularly mopping carpets can help to remove dust and dirt that even a regular vacuum cleaner will miss, which helps to keep your carpets fresher. I try to mop my carpets at least once a month to keep them looking their best, and I find the result comparable to the use of a steam cleaner when done regularly.

You can use almost any non-rinsing cleaner when you mop your carpets; test a non-conspicuous area before you use ANY cleaner on your carpet for safety, however. I generally use ammonia to clean my carpets because it is inexpensive and has a history of being used to clean carpets in ages past.

Just open a window to provide some ventilation while you are mopping!

The best time to mop your carpet is right after sweeping it; the sweeping will have removed most of the surface dirt and dislodged some of the ground-in dirt that you want to remove.

Carpet Mopping Solution

- 1 cup ammonia
- 1 gallon very warm water

Moisten your mop in this solution and wring it out slightly. You want it wet but not dripping for maximum effectiveness. Apply the mop in a sweeping motion to the carpet, rinsing the mop in the bucket regularly.

Change the cleaning solution when it becomes dirty to avoid transferring the dirt to other areas of the carpet.

Allow the carpet to dry and then sweep once again to remove any debris that was loosened by mopping for maximum cleanliness.

Borax

Borax has the added benefit of killing insects that come into contact with it. If you are concerned about insects you can leave a light sprinkling of borax on your carpets at all times by just sweeping it into the pile so that it will not be obvious. Just reapply after you sweep or mop your carpets.

Sprinkle borax in corners, around walls and anywhere insects hide to help curtail the bug population.

Borax Bug Solution

- 1/4 cup borax
- 1 gallon warm water

Use this solution to wash counters, cabinets, walls, floors and other surfaces of infected areas. Do not rinse. Insects will get the borax on their feet as they walk across the surfaces and die when they lick it off as they clean their feet.

This solution is not a cure-all but I recommend using it in addition to any other insect control methods you have available.

Octagon Soap

Octagon Soap is an old-fashioned soap currently produced by the Colgate-Palmolive company. This versatile soap can be used to clean all around your house--even your body--While you are starting over. I have even used it to wash my hair when it was shorter! One of the best features of this soap is the fact that you can safely wash dishes with it and save lots of money by not purchasing expensive dishwashing liquid!

Dishwashing

Place a bar of Octagon soap in one of your dish pans (or one side of your sink). Fill the sink to the desired water level with warm water, allowing the water to stream over the bar of Octagon soap.

Remove the bar and set aside. Place dirty dishes in the water and allow to soak while you fill the other dish pan (or the other side of the sink) with rinse water.

Take a cleaning rag or sponge and lather well using the bar of Octagon. Clean your dishes with the soap and rinse in the clear water. Place dishes on a layer of rags or towels until you finish the whole load and then hand dry.

TIP: A teaspoon of bleach in your rinse water will help to sanitize your dishes, especially if you let them soak in this solution for a few moments.

Homemade Dishwashing Liquid

If you prefer using dishwashing liquid to a bar of soap, you can make it yourself for a lot less than you can buy it in the store.

Ingredients
- 1/2 bar Octagon Soap, grated
- 1 Tablespoon Washing Soda
- 1 Gallon Water

Supplies
- 2 Quart saucepan
- Stove burner or hot plate
- Wooden spoon (stainless steel will work, but avoid aluminum)
- Empty gallon jug
- Empty squirt bottle (an old dishwashing liquid or shampoo bottle)
- Funnel (can cut the top off a soft drink bottle)

Pour a quart of water into the saucepan and place upon the stove burner. Turn the heat on medium and add your grated Octagon soap. Stir until the soap is completely dissolved.

Add the washing soda to the mixture and stir until well mixed. Add 1/2 gallon of cool water to the empty gallon jug and then pour the Octagon soap mixture into the jug.

Cap the jug and shake well to mix. Open the jug and top off with the remaining water. Pour this mixture into your empty squirt bottle and use like regular dishwashing liquid.

NOTE: This does not contain the artificial sudsing agents that most commercial dishwashing liquid contains so it does not create the volume of suds that you may be accustomed to. It really cleans well even without the suds, however!

If you would like to see a step by step video about making this dishwashing liquid, I have one available on YouTube[7] and will place the link in the References section.

General Cleaning

The commercials want to make it a lot more complicated than it is, but cleaning is one of the simplest things you can do. A little soap and water can do wonders!

- Octagon soap
- Gallon warm water
- Cleaning rags or sponge

Dip your rag or sponge into the water to moisten. Lather it up with Octagon soap and apply to the soiled area. Rinse with clean water when finished.

---

[7] http://www.youtube.com/watch?v=ge0CLqtbdAY

If you don't want to use Octagon soap you can use ammonia instead.

Laundry

At first you may need to wash your laundry by hand. Place the laundry in a pan of warm water. Rub Octagon soap into the wet clothing and work up a lather. Work the lather through the laundry by rubbing the items against each other to create friction. Pay special attention to stained areas to get them extra clean. Rinse well and hang to dry.

If you have access to a washing machine you 1 tablespoon of grated Octagon soap per load of water. Add 1 cup of ammonia to increase the cleaning power significantly at a lower price (and with less chemicals) than those commercial detergents available in the stores.

You can make a gallon of liquid laundry detergent at home for just a few cents that will clean just as well or better than that pricey stuff at the store:

Liquid Laundry Detergent

- 1/2 bar Octagon soap, grated
- 1 cup Borax
- 1 cup Washing Soda
- Gallon of water

- Empty gallon jug (1.5 gallon size recommended if available)

Place a quart of water into a saucepan and add the grated Octagon soap. Stir over medium heat until dissolved. Add the washing soda and borax and stir until well mixed. Pour approximately 1 quart of water into the empty gallon jug, and then add the Octagon solution. Cap and shake well to mix before topping off the jug with the remaining water. Use 1/2 cup for regularly soiled laundry, 3/4 cup for extra dirty loads.

Powdered Laundry Detergent

- 1/2 bar Octagon soap, grated
- 1 cup Borax
- 1 cup Washing Soda
- Empty container

Mix the ingredients together. Use 1 tablespoon for regular loads, 2 tablespoons for really dirty loads.

This recipe doesn't last as long as the liquid laundry detergent recipe, but when you use warm water it seems to clean better on really dirty loads of laundry.

Laundry Tips

For whites, add 1/2 cup of bleach to the washer before adding your clothes. Allow to agitate if possible for a minute before adding your laundry detergent for best results.

Use vinegar as a fabric softener and rinse aid. Add 1 cup to your final rinse to freshen and remove soap residue. Alternately, dilute commercial liquid fabric softener to 1/2 strength and use the lowest amount called for on the instructions. You will have the same amount of fabric softening power without the waste.

No matter how poor you think you are, sort your laundry in whites and colors. This step alone will keep your laundry looking better because it will prevent fading colors from turning your whites gray and keep white towel fuzz off of your dark clothing. You can wash colors (or whites) more often if needed, allowing the other to build up until you have a full load if you use the Laundromat.

Laundromats

There are several reasons why you will actually break even (if not come out ahead) by using a Laundromat as opposed to buying a washer and dryer.

- No initial expense for equipment.
- No need to worry about hauling the heavy appliances if you move.
- No need to have a washer/dryer hookup (or pay more for a rental that is equipped with hookups).
- Access to larger/better quality machines than you may be able to afford for your home.
- Can wash all of your laundry at once instead of taking all day to wash and dry numerous loads, saving a significant amount of time.
- No additional fees for the water/electric/gas usage-- it is all factored into the load fee at the Laundromat.

Commodes

Flush the commode. Add 1/2 cup of bleach to the bowl. Scrub all areas inside of the commode with the toilet brush. Allow to soak for maximum germ killing and cleaning. Flush when done.

Clean the outside of the commode with a mixture of 1/4 cup of bleach per gallon of water to kill germs and clean the surface. Do not rinse, and discard the rag or place in a safe spot until laundry day to avoid contaminating your laundry or creating bleach stains on your good clothes from contact with the bleach-saturated cloth.

Tubs and Showers

Clean tubs and showers with a basic ammonia solution (1/2 cup ammonia per gallon of water). Rings and soap buildup can be scrubbed away by making a paste with baking soda and ammonia. Rinse well.

Frankly, instead of making up the ammonia and baking soda mixture, I just scrub the tub or shower with a "Miracle" Eraser and warm water. It removes the scum easily and without the chemical smell. Rinse well to remove the remnants of the eraser.

Disinfect Surfaces

Disinfect any surface (countertops, sinks, etc.) with a solution of 1/4 cup bleach per gallon of water. Wipe or spray onto the surface and allow to air dry.

Life Goes On

The most important thing to remember in this journey is that life goes on. In a few years you will look back on this experience as an adventure and celebrate how you overcame yet another challenge.

Start out now looking at this like the adventure that it is. Enjoy the fact that you can camp out and grow in yet another dimension. Savor the fact that you can take this time to learn how to live on less than you ever thought possible.

Laugh when you pass those aisles upon aisles of stuff and know in your heart that you can buy it if you want, but that you *really* don't need it.

Pass on this information to someone else who may need it, and show them that they, like you, can start over on a shoestring.

References

Instead of distracting you with a bunch of links I will include all links and references in this one area, in alphabetical order. If you know of any resources aside from the ones I mention here please send me an email at annie@annienygma.com and I will be happy to include them in future editions. Thanks!

Adbrite: for advertising revenue on blogs and other websites:
http://adbrite.com

Arm and Hammer Washing Soda
http://www.greatcleaners.com/Products/Arm%20and%20Hammer/PID-33200-03020

Blogging websites (free):
http://blogger.com
http://www.wordpress.com

Cheap RV Living (for VanDwelling information):
http://cheaprvliving.com/index.html

Dishwashing Liquid video tutorial on YouTube:
http://www.youtube.com/watch?v=ge0CLqtbdAY

How to Write and Sell an Ebook Ebook:
http://www.smashwords.com/books/view/36647

MagicJack (VOIP phone for $20/year):
http://www.magicjack.com

Octagon Soap
http://www.amazon.com/Octagon-Purpose-Laundry-Soap-Colgate/dp/B000GCOLQ6

PayPal:
http://www.paypal.com

Survival Guide to Homelessness:
http://guide2homelessness.blogspot.com/

Living in a Van Without Getting Hassled:
http://www.rockinvan.com/slummin_it.html

Minimalist Cooking by Meg Wolfe:
https://www.e-junkie.com/ecom/gb.php?cl=135990&c=ib&aff=130414

Minimalist Wardrobe:
http://www.missminimalist.com/2011/03/the-minimalist-wardrobe-aka-the-10-item-wardrobe/

Mturk:
http://mturk.com/

The Minimalist Cleaning Method Book:
http://www.amazon.com/Minimalist-Cleaning-Method-Expanded-Supplies/dp/1479202290/ref=sr_1_1?s=books&ie=UTF8&qid=1350244413&sr=1-1&keywords=minimalist+cleaning+method

The Uniform Project:
http://www.theuniformproject.com/

Where to Work Online Ebook:
https://www.smashwords.com/books/view/36433

Yahoo Contributor Network:
https://contributor.yahoo.com/

About the Author

Annie Brewer is a frugal living expert who combines minimalism with frugality to be a stay at home single mom to her daughter. She is the author of the popular book <u>The Shoestring Girl: How I Live on Practically Nothing And YOU Can Too!</u>, <u>The Minimalist Cleaning Method Expanded Edition</u> and a number of other titles. You can learn more about her at Annienygma.com.

Personal circumstances gave Annie the opportunity to pack up her van and relocate to another part of Kentucky. She took this chance to give away all of her excess and completely start over. This book is the result of this experience.

Connect With Annie Online:

Main Website:
http://annienygma.com

Email:
annie@annienygma.com

Amazon Author Page:
http://www.amazon.com/author/annienygma

Facebook:
http://www.facebook.com/annienygma

Twitter:
http://www.twitter.com/annienygma

Yahoo! Contributor Network:
http://contributor.yahoo.com/user/annienygma

Smashwords:
http://www.smashwords.com/profile/view/annienyg
ma

THE SHOESTRING GIRL

How I Live on Practically Nothing... And YOU Can Too!

ANNIE BREWER

Do You Want to Live on Less?

Would you like to learn how from someone who actually does?

Over ten years ago I found myself a single mother with three children to raise.

I had to learn fast.

I had to support those kids on a fast food paycheck while I put myself through school.

Not only did I manage to do it but I topped my own expectations. We ended up living better than I <u>ever</u> would have imagined.

Since then I have not only quit my day job but I have built up sufficient income to become a single stay-at-home mother to my youngest child. This feat would not have been possible without the frugality of shoestring living.

We live well on about $500 a month - and know how to live on even LESS!

Over the years I have shared my secrets with others who have fallen on hard times. I have helped friends who became disabled, single parents, the unemployed and others who found a need to live on as little money as possible.

The first thing I always shared was the timeless words of my grandmother. Even now I can hear her reminding me to hold up my head because...

Annie Jean Brewer

"There's no sin in being poor!"

This may be your first brush with life below the poverty line. You may be scared. You may be ashamed. You may not know what to do or where to start.

I'm here to help you save money

I have drawn upon my 10+ years of personal experience to create the ultimate frugal living guide. I won't bore you with stupid fluff about clipping coupons. Instead, you will find a concise method you can implement to save thousands of dollars over the course of a year.

Sections Include:
Housing
Auto
Groceries (Includes raising food)
Computers (includes where to find free and inexpensive software)
Television (includes watching shows online for free)
Books (lots of links to free ebooks and how to search for free ebooks online)
Music (includes links for free music sites)
Clothing
Cleaning tips and recipes
Personal care tips and recipes
Furniture
Thrift Shops
Yard Sales
Jobs and self-employment
And much more!

I not only explain the exact methods that I use to save money and live frugally but I also explain how I could live on about <u>half</u> of the money that I actually do.

While you may not wish to apply everything here I am confident that you will be inspired to save more money than you ever thought possible. You will learn the skills you need to overcome your current financial challenge.

Start Saving Money Today!

Available in both print and ebook format at many popular retailers.

HOW TO WRITE EBOOKS FOR A LIVING

By

Annie Brewer

Do you Want to Earn a Living from Ebooks?

As a single mother I asked the question: *How can I stay at home with my child but still pay the bills?*

Job after job kept taking me away from my daughter's fleeting childhood. My frustration grew every time I missed another milestone in her life.

I combed the Internet in search of the answer. I found several places online where you could work from home but many of these kept me literally chained to a computer for hours on end. There had to be a better way!

One day I stumbled upon a blogger selling ebooks from his website. Not only selling them, he was actually earning his living from ebook sales!

"I can do that!" I thought.

I contacted him, buttered him up and picked his brain.

Gleefully following his instructions I finished my first ebook, published it online and drooled at the screen in anticipation.

I sat, I watched, I waited. After my first few sales the money dried up like a puddle in the desert.

What was I doing wrong?

I went out in search of more writers and picked a few more brains. I stayed up late at night researching and experimenting, determined to become a successful ebook writer. I refused to give up and quit.

I discovered the secret to ebook success.

Now I spend my days at home instead of at the dreaded day job. I take long walks with my daughter instead of punching a time clock. Money comes automatically now so I can relax and enjoy my life.

Anyone can make a living with ebooks, GUARANTEED

If you follow the steps in this guide you are **guaranteed** to earn money with ebooks. I am so convinced that you will be able to earn a living entirely from ebook sales that I offer you a **6-month money-back guarantee.** If after 6 months of applying this method you are not earning money from your ebooks send me a copy of your purchase receipt and I will refund your purchase price.

This guide teaches you:

- What equipment you need to write ebooks
- What bank accounts you need
- How to financially prepare to live off your ebook royalty income
- Where to find the time to write
- The importance of a blog
- Where to practice writing in preparation
- Where to find subjects to write about
- How to create your ebook
- Where and how to create an ebook cover
- Ebook descriptions
- Where to distribute your ebook
- Ebook pricing
- The importance of a backlist
- Social media
- Making the leap by quitting your day job
- ***And more!***

"A journey of a thousand miles begins with a single step." - Confucius.

Will you take that step today?

Where to Work Online

By

Annie Jean Brewer

Do you want to work at home?

There are so many scams out there it is hard to determine legitimate work at home jobs. It took me years of searching and I stumbled upon my first legitimate opportunity entirely by chance.

Since then I have learned how to work entirely from home and have compiled a list of legitimate work at home opportunities. There is a little here for everyone as well as tips to avoid getting ripped off by the scams out there.

This book shows you:
- The Golden Rule to working online
- Money Matters
- Multiple Income Streams
- Fast Cash
- Tinkering Cash
- Searching Cash
- Writing Cash
- Therapy Cash
- Affiliate Links
- Roll Your Own (ebook that is..)
- Phone Actresses
- "Official" Jobs
- Clearinghouses
- The Big List of Online Jobs
- *And more!*

If you are serious about working online, this is the only book you need.

"He that can live sparingly need not be rich."
Benjamin Franklin

There are a lot of frugality books out there.

I know. I've bought most of them.

Saving money isn't just a hobby for me; it is a way of life. It is what allows me to be a single stay-at-home mother for my child. We currently live on about $500 a month but if we wanted to we could easily live on **less.**

Here are just a few of the tips that I personally use to save thousands of dollars a year:

Tip #1 - Auto purchases. Annual Savings: $5,364.
Tip #32 - General Cleaning. Annual Savings: $216.
Tip #45 - Carpet cleaning. Annual Savings: $100.
Tip #67 - Salvaging stained clothing. Annual Savings: $50.
Tip #78 - Printer ink. Annual Savings: $100.
Tip #89 - Software. Annual Savings: $200
Tip #95 - Movies. Annual Savings: $52
Tip #100 - Television. Annual Savings: $1,200
Tip #114 - Credit Cards. Annual Savings: $480
Tip #129 - Where to work for Maximum savings. Annual savings: $1,011
Tip #241 - Housing. Annual Savings: $3,600

What could you do with that much extra money?

Written by the author of <u>The Shoestring Girl: How I Live on Practically Nothing and You Can Too</u>, this guide covers:

- Auto
- Cleaning
- Computers
- Entertainment
- Finance
- Food
- Gardening
- General Household
- Housing
- Kids
- Personal Care
- Pets
- Shopping
- Travel
- Utilities
- Funeral expenses
- *And more*

Minus the fluff, this nitty-gritty guide immediately gets down to the business of saving money with *over 400 unique tips* designed to help anyone with a desire to save money.

You may not choose to use all of the frugal ideas in this guide but I am confident that this book will inspire you to **save more money** than you ever thought possible.

How Much Can YOU save?

Annie has not paid for a cable subscription in over a decade. Instead her family watches videos online for free. In this book she shares her tips, tricks and online wisdom to teach others how they can do the same.

This book covers:
• How to protect your computer before you start
• What software you need
• A list of video websites
• How to search for more websites
• What to do when your favorite site disappears
• Video viewing tips
• How to deal with Popups and other ads
• How to buffer videos
• How to manually cache videos
• Website registration cautions
• Why not to pay for using these sites
• Torrents
• File Sharing programs
• *And more!*

Readers will not only have a resource of links to get started with but will learn how to discover even more viewing opportunities online and how to maximize their video experience while saving money in the process.

CONGRATULATIONS YOU HAVE REACHED
THE END!
Thank you for your support!

***

Please help others—review this book.

31482028R00065

Made in the USA
Middletown, DE
02 May 2016